I0428818

CONTENTS

CORE EXPECTATIONS
FOR PEACE CORPS VOLUNTEERS

In working toward fulfilling the Peace Corps Mission of promoting world peace and friendship, as a trainee and Volunteer, you are expected to:

1. Prepare your personal and professional life to make a commitment to serve abroad for a full term of 27 months

2. Commit to improving the quality of life of the people with whom you live and work; and, in doing so, share your skills, adapt them, and learn new skills as needed

3. Serve where the Peace Corps asks you to go, under conditions of hardship, if necessary, and with the flexibility needed for effective service

4. Recognize that your successful and sustainable development work is based on the local trust and confidence you build by living in, and respectfully integrating yourself into, your host community and culture

5) Recognize that you are responsible 24 hours a day, 7 days a week for your personal conduct and professional performance

6. Engage with host country partners in a spirit of cooperation, mutual learning, and respect

7. Work within the rules and regulations of the Peace Corps and the local and national laws of the country where you serve

8. Exercise judgment and personal responsibility to protect your health, safety, and well-being and that of others

9. Recognize that you will be perceived, in your host country and community, as a representative of the people, cultures, values, and traditions of the United States of America

10. Represent responsively the people, cultures, values, and traditions of your host country and community to people in the United States both during and following your service

PEACE CORPS/BOTSWANA
HISTORY AND PROGRAMS

History of the Peace Corps in Botswana

The Peace Corps entered the Republic of Botswana, formerly known as Bechuanaland, in December 1966, just two months after the country gained independence. Botswana's emergence as an independent nation heightened the need for a skilled labor force. More than 1,800 Peace Corps Volunteers served in Botswana from 1966 to 1997. Peace Corps projects contributed to nearly every sector of Botswana's development, including education, health, environment, urban planning, and economics. Volunteers filled significant gaps in the labor force and, in many cases, made singular contributions to the development of Botswana. There are scores of leading figures in Botswana who have a Peace Corps connection, be it as a co-worker, teacher, or friend.

Since its independence in 1966, Botswana progressed from being one of the world's poorest countries to one of the few developing nations to reach middle-income status. The country's per capita income has grown rapidly. Life expectancy at birth increased from 48 years to over 60 years. Formal sector employment grew from 14,000 jobs to 120,000. Moreover, the nation's infrastructure, including roads, power generation, schools, health facilities, and housing, increased dramatically. Partly due to Botswana's remarkable economic transition, the Peace Corps withdrew from the country in 1997.

In 2003, the Peace Corps returned to Botswana at the request of former President Festus Mogae, who recognized that AIDS was starting to erode the prodigious steady development advances realized in the country since independence.

History and Future of Peace Corps Programming in Botswana

Botswana's HIV infection rate is one of the highest in the world. The government, under the leadership of former President Mogae, has publicly acknowledged the crisis, implemented a National AIDS Council and Coordinating Agency, and developed a national plan called the National Strategic Framework for HIV/AIDS.

The National AIDS Coordinating Agency (NACA) asked Peace Corps/Botswana to focus on capacity-building. Volunteers work in four programs based in:

1. Schools: Volunteers facilitate the implementation of the Life Skills curriculum and serve to link teachers/school officials and the community.

2. Community-based/nongovernmental organizations (NGOs): Volunteers build organizational and staff capacity in management, programming, resource use, and fundraising.

3. Clinics and District Health Management Teams (CHT): Volunteers increase awareness of HIV/AIDS and prevention, develop community support groups, work with youth, build technical capacity, and increase participation in government programs.

4. Local Government Capacity Building Volunteers work in District AIDS coordinators' (DACs) offices and Social and Community Development (S&CD) offices: Volunteers build capacity in program planning, implementation, monitoring/evaluation, and mobilization of government and community responses to HIV/AIDS.

COUNTRY OVERVIEW:
BOTSWANA AT A GLANCE

History

By about 1700, the ancestors of today's Batswana (citizens) were established as self-sufficient herders, farmers, and hunters. Their first contact with Europeans was through missionaries in the early 19th century. After hostilities broke out between the Batswana and expansionist Afrikaners from South Africa in the last quarter of that century, the tribal chiefs asked the British for assistance. The British responded and, in 1885, proclaimed a protectorate in what was then called Bechuanaland. They retained colonial control until 1966. Bechuanaland played a prominent role in the British penetration of Central Africa in the 19th century. Cecil Rhodes called the region the "Suez Canal to the north" and considered it vital to his plans for territorial expansion. British interests in Bechuanaland were primarily strategic, and internal affairs were handled with more or less benign neglect.

Under British authority, local tribal governments were allowed to continue, with chiefs retaining much of their authority. With the establishment of separate advisory councils representing Africans and Europeans in 1920, the evolution of modern self-government began. In 1951, a joint advisory council was formed, consisting of both European and African members. Over the years these advisory bodies were consulted on a constantly expanding range of matters.

By 1964 the British were prepared to accept a system of internal self-government. Seretse Khama, the British-educated heir to the chieftainship of the Bangwato (which he forfeited) and a former enemy of the British Empire, was elected as the first prime minister and, subsequently, first president. He is revered for his nonpartisan politics and for leading the country to full independence in 1966. Botswana has had orderly presidential transitions, beginning with Quett Ketumile Masire, who followed Khama, then Festus Mogae, and currently Lt. General Seretse Khama Ian Khama (son of the first president), who took office on April 1, 2008.

Government

Botswana is a multiparty democracy with a stable and progressive political climate. The Constitution established a unicameral National Assembly, now composed of 57 members directly elected by popular vote, four members elected by the assembly, and the attorney general. The chief executive is the president, who is chosen by his party. Presidents serve up to two five-year terms. The president selects the cabinet ministers and the vice president from the National Assembly. The Constitution provides for freedom of speech, press, and religion, contributing to Botswana's reputation for being one of Africa's most stable countries.

Botswana has three main political parties and numerous minor parties. National politics has been dominated by the Botswana Democratic Party (BDP), which has won every presidential election since independence.

Economy

Botswana maintained one of the world's highest economic growth rates since independence in 1966. Through fiscal discipline and sound management, the nation transformed itself from one of the poorest countries to a middle-income country (per capita GDP of $16,600 in 2012). While there have been major reductions in poverty levels of Botswana citizens since independence, there is still high unemployment (approximately 18 percent) and a gap between those participating fully in the economy and many who do not.

Botswana's mining industry includes nickel (second largest producer in Africa) and diamonds (with the second/third largest diamond pipes in the world), among other elements. Other economic activities include tourism and agriculture, especially beef production.

The government has managed the country's resources prudently and kept recurrent expenditures within its revenue, allowing for investment in infrastructure and services. HIV/AIDS has affected the development gains and impacts all aspects of Batswana life.

People and Culture

The population includes no fewer than 20 African ethnic groups and a small population of peoples of Indian and European descent. In the colonial period, white settlement in Botswana consisted mainly of Afrikaners and English who settled on border farms. Since then, a larger expatriate population from Europe, North America (including former Peace Corps Volunteers), South Asia, and elsewhere in Africa (e.g., Zimbabwe, Tanzania, Nigeria, Kenya) has been drawn to the country. Much of this immigration is the result of Botswana's continued reliance on foreign skilled labor, particularly in the medical sector.

Although there are distinct linguistic and cultural differences among Botswana's ethnic groups, the majority of the population (79 percent) is Tswana, whose ethnic dominance in Botswana dates from the eight Tswana states that ruled most of the area in the 19th century. The populations of these states were given the official status of "tribes" under British colonial rule, and the term is still used commonly today. The name Botswana is derived from the Tswana. The official language is English and the national language is Setswana; both are widely spoken.

Botswana is predominantly Christian, but many religions are represented in larger towns. The two most active and popular churches are the Zion Christian Church and the Roman Catholic Church. There are also numerous smaller denominations throughout the country. Although Christianity is widely practiced, so too are indigenous religions. Interestingly, there are fewer than 500 Western-educated doctors in the country, while there are more than 5,000 practicing traditional healers.

Environment

Botswana is one of Africa's least densely populated countries, with a population of approximately 2.1 million people in a land area slightly smaller than Texas. It is known for unforgettable wilderness, the spectacular waterways of the Okavango Delta, the Kalahari sand dunes, and an abundance of wildlife. Much of the country is flat, with gentle undulations and occasional rocky outcrops.

Of the 2.1 million Batswana, UNAIDS estimated that close to one of four adults ages 15-49 were HIV positive in 2009. National sentinel surveillance determined that one of three pregnant women was HIV positive. Currently, about 320,000 adults and children are estimated to be HIV positive and 150,000 are in need of anti-retroviral therapy (ART). (Most who need ART are on it.) AIDS orphans are estimated at 52,000. The long-term impact of the epidemic is that by 2021, the government has projected that the population in Botswana will be 18 percent lower than it would have been in the absence of the epidemic. In addition, despite the longer life expectancy for patients receiving antiretroviral (ARV) therapy, the number of deaths is expected to rise and nearly double by 2016.

RESOURCES FOR FURTHER INFORMATION

Following is a list of websites for additional information about the Peace Corps and Botswana and to connect you to returned Volunteers and other invitees. Please keep in mind that although we try to make sure all these links are active and current, we cannot guarantee it. If you do not have access to the Internet, visit your local library. Libraries offer free Internet usage and often let you print information to take home.

A note of caution: As you surf the Internet, be aware that you may find bulletin boards and chat rooms in which people are free to express opinions about the Peace Corps based on their own experience, including comments by those who were unhappy with their choice to serve in the Peace Corps. These opinions are not those of the Peace Corps or the U.S. government, and we hope you will keep in mind that no two people experience their service in the same way.

General Information About Botswana

http://en.wikipedia.org/wiki/Botswana
Wikipedia information on Botswana

www.countrywatch.com/
On this site, you can learn anything from what time it is in the Gaborone to how to convert from the dollar to the Botswana Pula. Just click on Botswana and go from there.

www.lonelyplanet.com/destinations
Visit this site for general travel advice about almost any country in the world.

www.state.gov
The State Department's website issues background notes periodically about countries around the world. Find Botswana and learn more about its social and political history. You can also go to the site's international travel section to check on conditions that may affect your safety.

www.geography.about.com/library/maps/blindex.htm
This online world atlas includes maps and geographical information, and each country page contains links to other sites, such as the Library of Congress, that contain comprehensive historical, social, and political background.

www.cyberschoolbus.un.org
This United Nations site allows you to search for statistical information for member states of the U.N.

Connect With Returned Volunteers and Other Invitees

www.rpcv.org
This is the site of the National Peace Corps Association, made up of returned Volunteers. On this site you can find links to all the Web pages of the "Friends of" groups for most countries of service, comprised of former Volunteers who served in those countries. There are also regional groups that frequently get together for social events and local volunteer activities.

www.PeaceCorpsWorldwide.org
This site is hosted by a group of returned Volunteer writers. It is a monthly online publication of essays and Volunteer accounts of their Peace Corps service.

Online Articles/Current News Sites About Botswana

www.gazette.bw

The website of *The Botswana Gazette*, a weekly newspaper based in Gaborone

www.gov.bw

The website of the government of Botswana offers daily news articles.

www.mmegi.bw

The website of *Mmegi*, a newspaper based in Gaborone.

www.mg.co.za/

The *Mail & Guardian* of South Africa contains articles of regional interest.

http://allafrica.com/botswana/

African news and information for a global audience.

International Development Sites About Botswana

www.usaid.gov

U.S. Agency for International Development

www.unaids.org

Joint United Nations Programme on HIV/AIDS

www.undp.org

United Nations Development Programme

Recommended Books

1. Dow, Unity and Essex, Max. *Saturday is for Funerals* Harvard University Press, 2009.

2. Allison, Peter. *Whatever You Do, Don't Run: True Tales of a Botswana Safari Guide*. The Lyons Press, 2007.

3. Alverson, Marianne. *Under African Sun*. Chicago: University of Chicago Press, 1987.

4. Denbow, James and Phenyo C. Thebe. *Culture and Customs of Botswana*. Greenwood Press, 2006.

5. Epstein, Helen. *The Invisible Cure: Why We Are Losing the Fight Against AIDS in Africa*. Picador, 2008

6. Head, Bessie. *When Rain Clouds Gather*. Portsmouth, N.H.: Heinemann, 1996.

7. Nolen, Stephanie. *28 Stories of AIDS in Africa*. Walker & Company, 2007

8. Rush, Norman. *Whites: Stories*. New York, N.Y.: Vintage Books, 1992.

9. Smith, Alexander McCall. *The No. 1 Ladies' Detective Agency*. New York, N.Y.: Anchor Books/Random House. 1998.

10. Williams, Susan. *The Colour Bar: The Triumph of Seretse Khama and His Nation*. Penguin Group (U.S.), 2008.

Books About the History of the Peace Corps

1. Hoffman, Elizabeth Cobbs. *All You Need is Love: The Peace Corps and the Spirit of the 1960s*. Cambridge, Mass.: Harvard University Press, 2000.

2. Rice, Gerald T. *The Bold Experiment: JFK's Peace Corps*. Notre Dame, Ind.: University of Notre Dame Press, 1985.

3. Stossel, Scott. *Sarge: The Life and Times of Sargent Shriver*. Washington, D.C.: Smithsonian Institution Press, 2004.

4. Meisler, Stanley. *When the World Calls: The Inside Story of the Peace Corps and its First 50 Years*. Boston, Mass.: Beacon Press, 2011.

Books on the Volunteer Experience

1. Dirlam, Sharon. *Beyond Siberia: Two Years in a Forgotten Place*. Santa Barbara, Calif.: McSeas Books, 2004.

2. Casebolt, Marjorie DeMoss. *Margarita: A Guatemalan Peace Corps Experience*. Gig Harbor, Wash.: Red Apple Publishing, 2000.

3. Erdman, Sarah. *Nine Hills to Nambonkaha: Two Years in the Heart of an African Village*. New York, N.Y.: Picador, 2003.

4. Hessler, Peter. *River Town: Two Years on the Yangtze*. New York, N.Y.: Perennial, 2001.

5. Kennedy, Geraldine ed. *From the Center of the Earth: Stories out of the Peace Corps*. Santa Monica, Calif.: Clover Park Press, 1991.

6. Thompsen, Moritz. *Living Poor: A Peace Corps Chronicle*. Seattle, Wash.: University of Washington Press, 1997 (reprint).

LIVING CONDITIONS AND VOLUNTEER LIFESTYLE

Communications

Mail

Postal rates in Botswana are reasonable and airmail to the United States generally takes about two weeks. Mail supplies can be purchased at all post office branches. Sending large packages via airmail can be very expensive, but smaller items, such as photographs or CDs, can be sent for a reasonable fee. Airmail from the U.S. to Botswana takes two to four weeks while surface mail takes four to six weeks to arrive. Advise your family and friends to keep all documentation related to the packages they send to Botswana so any package that does not arrive can be traced. Most mail will come with a tracking number that can be tracked online and will show when a package from the U.S. clears customs in Botswana. Postal insurance is a good idea when sending packages from the United States.

During pre-service training, your mail should be sent to the Peace Corps office address (PCT Name, c/o Peace Corps Botswana, Private Bag 00243, Gaborone, Botswana). The Peace Corps staff will then forward your mail to the training site.

After training, you will give your family and friends the address of your site of assignment to avoid lengthy delays in transferring from the Peace Corps office to your final location.

Telephones

Domestic and international phone service is available throughout Botswana. Service is more expensive than in the United States, particularly for international calls. While there are few public phone booths, individuals offering phone services can be found in nearly every corner of small towns and villages. The Peace Corps purchases a cellphone for each Volunteer in-country (for less than $30, although ones with additional features can cost considerably more). The network covers most towns and larger villages. Many friends and family members in the U.S. purchase low cost international dialing plans to contact a Volunteer in Botswana or use Skype or similar systems for communicating with a Volunteer.

Computer, Internet, and Email Access

Most larger villages and towns in Botswana have internet cafes. Your access to email will be limited during the nine weeks of pre-service training because email is not always readily available at the training site and training is time-consuming. You should be able to access email at an internet cafe during off-hours and on weekends. At your site placement for two years, you may not have regular internet access. Some Volunteers, approximately 25 percent, only access the internet once a month when they visit a larger nearby village for grocery shopping.

Housing and Site Location

Your housing is provided by the government of Botswana or other partner organizations. Because of the wide range of housing in Botswana, there is considerable variation in Volunteer living situations. **You should come prepared to accept the Peace Corps' minimum standard for housing—a single room that is clean and can be secured with a lock, with access to clean water and sanitary bathroom and cooking space.** Electricity and piped-in water are not required by the Peace Corps.

Volunteers placed at the district level can expect fairly comfortable housing, which typically means a one- or two-bedroom cement house with a kitchen, indoor plumbing, and electricity. Volunteers based at the village level can expect housing to be more rustic, perhaps a room in a family compound in which services are limited or nonexistent. The government or partner organization is responsible for providing limited furnishings (bed, table, chair,) and covering the cost of utilities (cooking gas, water).

Living Allowance and Money Management

The Peace Corps provides each Volunteer with a small "walk-around" allowance during PST, a settling-in allowance to cover some of the minimal costs of setting up a new home, and a monthly living allowance that is intended to cover basic expenses. In addition, you will be paid a leave allowance equal to $24 per month and a travel allowance for Peace Corps-related trips (e.g., trips to the capital for medical care, meetings, etc.). All allowances are paid in local currency. The living allowance is deposited directly into your bank account (which you will set up before completion of pre-service training) on a monthly basis.

Volunteers are expected to live modestly. The living allowance supports a very simple lifestyle and does not include money for things like weekly trips to the movies or phone calls home.

Food and Diet

The absence of basic food items is not an issue in Botswana. In fact, Volunteers may be surprised to find a large variety of English and American products, such as Heinz ketchup, Hellmann's mayonnaise, and Doritos chips, although all might not be accessible on the Volunteer living allowance or at your site. Fresh fruits and vegetables are available, even in outlying areas, although variety may be quite limited. Access to specialty foods and grocery stores does vary according to one's placement. Those posted to district-level villages or large towns will be able to buy food items in their immediate vicinity. Those posted to villages, particularly in very rural spots, will be limited to periodic shopping trips in the larger towns.

The traditional diet in Botswana relies heavily on meat and starches (notably corn or maize, beans, rice, potatoes, and sorghum). Starches are usually served in a stew or with gravy, made of vegetables like cabbages, tomatoes, greens, and onions. Beetroot and butternut often give color to a dish.

Committed vegetarians will find it relatively easy to maintain their diet but will have to find a way to convince meat-loving Batswana of the healthiness of their choice. Note that consumption of meat is given particular importance in some cultural celebrations.

Transportation

In general, it is not difficult to get around in Botswana. Common and inexpensive forms of public transportation include buses and private taxis. Buses travel on a fairly regular schedule throughout the country, although transfers may be necessary to reach one's destination. Buses range in size from combis (10- to 12-seat minivans) to large luxury buses (similar to Greyhound). While most transportation is reliable, the Peace Corps encourages Volunteers to assess the condition of both the vehicle and the driver before boarding.

The Peace Corps' recommended mode of transportation among Volunteer sites and the capital is a large bus and Volunteers' travel allowances reflect the slightly higher cost for this service.

Geography and Climate

In the northwest, the Okavango River drains inland from Angola to form the Okavango Delta. In the central northeast is a large area of hardpan plains bordering the Makgadikgadi pans. In the east, adjacent to the Limpopo drainage system, the land rises above 3,960 feet (1,200 meters), and the Limpopo Valley gradually descends from 2,970 feet (900 meters) in the south to 1,650 feet (500 meters) at its confluence with the Shashe River. This eastern region, which straddles the north-south railway line, has a somewhat less harsh climate and more fertile soil than elsewhere; it is here that most Batswana live. The rest of Botswana is covered with the thick sand (up to 396 feet, or 120 meters, deep) of the Kgalagadi (or Kalahari) Desert, which accounts for more than two-thirds of Botswana's land area. The Kgalagadi supports a vegetation of scrub and grasses, but there is an almost complete absence of surface water.

The country is largely arid or semiarid, and average rainfall ranges from 26 inches (650 millimeters) in the extreme northeast to less than 10 inches (250 millimeters) in the extreme southwest. Almost all the rainfall—consisting primarily of localized showers and thunderstorms—occurs during the summer months (October to April). Average daily maximum temperatures range from 72 degrees Fahrenheit (22 degrees Celsius) in July to 91 F (33 C) in January. However, the extremes range widely, from less than 23 F (-5 C) up to 109 F (43 C). The lowest temperatures are in the southwest, where early morning frost can occur from June to August.

Social Activities

In fulfillment of the three goals of the Peace Corps, Volunteers are expected to make their host communities the center of their social life and to stay at their sites unless they are traveling for approved vacation or work purposes. The types of activities and relationships that constitute a social life will vary according to a Volunteer's own interests and site assignment. Those in more urban settings will find a host of facilities, organizations, and other social outlets. Those in more rural settings may find limited formal social structures; in such cases, host families and friends in the community often become the center around which social activity revolves.

Professionalism, Dress, and Behavior

Batswana place great importance on conservative and professional dress in the workplace. The norms of professional dress mean slacks, shirts, and usually ties for men and dresses/skirts or nice pants for women. Ties are required of men in schools. Women are expected to wear skirts and men expected to wear jackets in the *kgotla*, which is the traditional chief's meeting place in every town or village. It is seen as a sign of respect for others when you dress professionally, and how you are viewed by your colleagues will be highly dependent on the way you present yourself. Tennis shoes, sneakers, or Teva-type sandals are not appropriate footwear for work. Although jeans and T-shirts are acceptable as casual wear, it is more common to see men wearing shirts with collars and casual slacks and women wearing skirts or slacks with blouses or casual dresses during non-work hours. Although shorts may be appropriate at home, most males wear long pants outdoors, even in summer months.

Sleeveless tops with spaghetti straps, tank tops, and low-cut tops are not appropriate for women outside the capital and larger towns. However, many Volunteers choose to wear tank tops inside their homes, particularly during the hot summer months.

All Volunteers should bring at least one business outfit (i.e., a suit or jacket and tie for men; a long, conservative dress or skirt for women). There will be occasions that bring Volunteers face-to-face with senior diplomats, traditional authorities, and civil servants, for which professional dress is expected.

Personal Safety

More detailed information about the Peace Corps' approach to safety is contained in the "Health Care and Safety" chapter, but it is an important issue and cannot be overemphasized. As stated in the Volunteer Handbook, becoming a Peace Corps Volunteer entails certain safety risks. Living and traveling in an unfamiliar environment (oftentimes alone), having a limited understanding of local language and culture, and being perceived as well-off are some of the factors that can put a Volunteer at risk. Many Volunteers experience varying degrees of unwanted attention and harassment. Petty thefts and burglaries are not uncommon, and incidents of physical and sexual assault do occur, although most Botswana Volunteers complete their two years of service without incident. The Peace Corps has established procedures and policies designed to help you reduce your risks and enhance your safety and security. These procedures and policies, in addition to safety training, will be provided once you arrive in Botswana. Using these tools, you are expected to take responsibility for your safety and well-being.

Each staff member at the Peace Corps is committed to providing Volunteers with the support they need to successfully meet the challenges they will face to have a safe, healthy, and productive service. We encourage Volunteers and families to look at our safety and security information on the Peace Corps website at **www.peacecorps.gov/safety**.

Information on these pages gives messages on Volunteer health and Volunteer safety. There is a section titled "Safety and Security —Our Partnership." Among topics addressed are the risks of serving as a Volunteer, posts' safety support systems, and emergency planning and communications.

Rewards and Frustrations

Invariably, Volunteers who have completed their service speak of the relationships they have established as the highlight of their service. Many speak of how they have learned to value and respect a more family- and community-centered way of life and of how they have grown in patience and understanding. Most are able to point to specific contributions they have made to a country's development. In Botswana, such contributions might include increasing the dialogue about HIV/AIDS, promoting the use of HIV/AIDS programs and services, seeing co-workers adopt new ways of accomplishing their jobs with an increase in productivity and effectiveness, decreasing stigma and discrimination against people with HIV/AIDS, and helping organizations develop and implement HIV/AIDS programs. Such positive reflections are the endpoint of a series of highs and lows that are part and parcel of the process of leaving the United States, entering Botswana, and adapting to the practices and pace of life in a new culture.

You will have less guidance and direction than you would get in a new job in the United States. Things will undoubtedly move at a much slower pace than you are accustomed to. You will probably need to make a paradigm shift from the American orientation toward tangible results to the Batswana love for a consultative process and protocol. To succeed in this environment, you will need a high degree of patience, self-confidence, creativity, and flexibility. If you do not deal well with gray areas, Botswana is probably not a good match for you. But if you come with a healthy respect for the process of being a Peace Corps Volunteer, as well as a desire to make tangible changes, you will have an incredible experience.

PEACE CORPS TRAINING

Pre-Service Training

Pre-service training is the first event within a competency-based training program that continues throughout your 27 months of service in Botswana. Pre-service training ensures that Volunteers are equipped with the knowledge, skills, and attitudes to effectively integrate into their communities and workplaces. The pre-service training experience provides an opportunity not only for the Peace Corps to assess a trainee's competence, but for trainees to re-evaluate their commitment to serve for 27 months to improve the quality of life of the people with whom Volunteers live and work and, in doing so, develop new knowledge, skills, and attitudes while adapting existing ones.

Peace Corps/Botswana's competencies are designed to be accomplished throughout the Volunteer's 27 months of learning. A trainee may not be able to complete all learning objectives for a competency during pre-service training; however, he or she must show adequate progress toward achieving the competencies in order to become a Volunteer[1]. Botswana's core competencies include the following:

- Build organization and individual capacity
- Integrate into your community
- Own your service
- Understand HIV/AIDS

Pre-service training is conducted in Botswana and directed by the Peace Corps with participation from representatives of Botswana organizations, current and former Volunteers, and/or training contractors. The length of pre-service training is nine weeks. . Botswana measures achievement of learning and determines if trainees have successfully achieved competencies, including language learner standards, for swearing in as a Peace Corps Volunteer.

Throughout service, Volunteers strive to achieve performance competencies. Initially, pre-service training affords the opportunity for trainees to develop and test their own resources. As a trainee, you will play an active role in self-education. You will be asked to decide how best to set and meet objectives and to find alternative solutions. You will be asked to prepare for an experience in which you will often have to take the initiative and accept responsibility for decisions. The success of your learning will be enhanced by your own effort to take responsibility for your learning and through sharing experiences with others.

Peace Corps training is founded on adult learning methods and often includes experiential "hands-on" applications such as conducting a participatory community needs assessment and facilitating groups. Successful training results in competence in various technical, linguistic, cross-cultural, health, and safety and security areas. Integrating into the community is usually one of the core competencies Volunteers strive to achieve both in pre-service training and during the first several months of service. Successful sustainable development work is based on the local trust and confidence Volunteers build by living in, and respectfully integrating into, the Botswana community and culture. Trainees are prepared for this through a homestay experience, which often requires trainees to live with host families during pre-service training. Integration into the community not only facilitates good working relationships, but it fosters language learning and cross-cultural acceptance and trust, which help ensure your health, safety, and security.

Woven into the competencies, setting trainees on the path to be able to communicate in the host country language is critical to being an effective Peace Corps Volunteer. So basic is this precept that it is spelled out in the Peace Corps Act: No person shall be assigned to duty as a Volunteer under this act in any foreign country or area unless at the time of such assignment he (or she) possesses such reasonable proficiency as his (or her) assignment requires in speaking the language of the country or area to which he (or she) is assigned.

Technical Training

Technical training will prepare you to work in Botswana by building on the skills you already have and helping you develop new skills in a manner appropriate to the needs of the country. The Peace Corps staff, Botswana experts, and current Volunteers will conduct the training program. Training places great emphasis on learning how to transfer the skills you have to the community in which you will serve as a Volunteer.

Technical training will include sessions on the general economic and political environment in Botswana and strategies for working within such a framework. You will review your technical sector's goals and will meet with the Botswana agencies and organizations that invited the Peace Corps to assist them. You will be supported and evaluated throughout the training to build the confidence and skills you need to undertake your project activities and be a productive member of your community.

Language Training

As a Peace Corps Volunteer, you will find that language skills are key to personal and professional satisfaction during your service. These skills are critical to your job performance, they help you integrate into your community, and they can ease your personal adaptation to the new surroundings. Therefore, language training is at the heart of the training program. You must successfully meet minimum language learner requirements to complete training and become a Volunteer. Botswana language instructors teach formal language classes 5-6 days a week in small groups of four to five people.

Your language training will incorporate a community-based approach. In addition to classroom time, you will be given assignments to work on outside of the classroom and with your host family. The goal is to get you to a point of basic social communication skills so you can practice and develop language skills further once you are at your site. Prior to being sworn in as a Volunteer, you will work on strategies to continue language studies during your service.

Cross-Cultural Training

As part of your pre-service training, you will live with a Botswana host family. This experience is designed to ease your transition to life at your site. Families go through an orientation conducted by Peace Corps staff to explain the purpose of pre-service training and to assist them in helping you adapt to living in Botswana. Many Volunteers form strong and lasting friendships with their host families.

Cross-cultural and community development training will help you improve your communication skills and understand your role as a facilitator of development. You will be exposed to topics such as community mobilization, conflict resolution, gender and development, nonformal and adult education strategies, and political structures.

Health Training

During pre-service training, you will be given basic medical training and information. You will be expected to practice preventive health care and to take responsibility for your own health by adhering to all medical policies. Trainees are required to attend all medical sessions. The topics include preventive health measures and minor and major medical issues that you might encounter while in Botswana. Nutrition, mental health, setting up a safe living compound, and how to avoid HIV/AIDS and other sexually transmitted diseases (STDs) are also covered.

Safety Training

During the safety training sessions, you will learn how to adopt a lifestyle that reduces your risks at home, at work, and during your travels. You will also learn appropriate, effective strategies for coping with unwanted attention and about your individual responsibility for promoting safety throughout your service.

Additional Trainings During Volunteer Service

In its commitment to institutionalize quality training, the Peace Corps has implemented a training system that provides Volunteers with continual opportunities to examine their commitment to Peace Corps service while increasing their technical and cross-cultural skills. During service, there are usually three training events. The titles and objectives for those trainings are as follows:

- In-service training: *Provides an opportunity for Volunteers to upgrade their technical, language, and project development skills while sharing their experiences and reaffirming their commitment after having served for three to six months.*

- Midterm conference (done in conjunction with technical sector in-service): *Assists Volunteers in reviewing their first year, reassessing their personal and project objectives, and planning for their second year of service.*

- Close-of-service conference: *Prepares Volunteers for the future after Peace Corps service and reviews their respective projects and personal experiences.*

The number, length, and design of these trainings are adapted to country-specific needs and conditions. The key to the training system is that training events are integrated and interrelated, from the pre-departure orientation through the end of your service, and are planned, implemented, and evaluated cooperatively by the training staff, Peace Corps staff, and Volunteers.

YOUR HEALTH CARE AND
SAFETY IN BOTSWANA

The Peace Corps' highest priority is maintaining the good health and safety of every Volunteer. Peace Corps medical programs emphasize the preventive, rather than the curative, approach to disease. The Peace Corps in Botswana maintains a clinic with a full-time medical officer and nurse, who takes care of Volunteers' primary health care needs. Additional medical services, such as testing and basic treatment, are also available in Botswana at local hospitals. If you become seriously ill, you will be transported either to an American-standard medical facility in the region or to the United States.

Health Issues in Botswana

Health conditions in Botswana are quite good. The most common health problems are related to the climate, which at times is very hot and dry and in winter can be colder than you may expect. Such preventive measures as a good diet, adequate hydration, and being alert to changes in your body are more important here than at home. Most villages have health posts or clinics, with hospitals in the larger villages and towns. Hospitals in the capital have good facilities. HIV/AIDS is a major health and development problem in the region, as Botswana's HIV infection rate is one of the highest in the world. Infection with HIV is preventable, however, if one avoids risky behavior.

Helping You Stay Healthy

The Peace Corps will provide you with all the necessary inoculations, medications, and information to stay healthy. Upon your arrival in Botswana, you will receive a medical handbook and a medical kit with supplies to take care of mild illnesses and first aid needs. The contents of the kit are listed later in this chapter.

During pre-service training, you will have access to basic medical supplies through the medical officer. However, you will be responsible for your own supply of prescription drugs and any other specific medical supplies you require, as the Peace Corps will not order these items during training. Please bring a three-month supply of any prescription drugs you use, since they may not be available here and it may take several months for shipments to arrive.

You will have physicals at midservice and at the end of your service. If you develop a serious medical problem during your service, the medical officers in Botswana will consult with the Office of Medical Services in Washington, D.C. If it is determined that your condition cannot be treated in Botswana, you may be sent out of the country for further evaluation and care.

Maintaining Your Health

As a Volunteer, you must accept considerable responsibility for your own health. Proper precautions will significantly reduce your risk of serious illness or injury. The adage "An ounce of prevention ..." becomes extremely important in areas where diagnostic and treatment facilities are not up to the standards of the United States. The most important of your responsibilities in Botswana is to take the following preventive measures:

- Malaria prophylaxis

- Precautions to prevent HIV/AIDS transmission

- Safe transportation choices

Many illnesses that afflict Volunteers worldwide are entirely preventable if proper food and water precautions are taken. These illnesses include food poisoning, parasitic infections, hepatitis A, dysentery, Guinea worms, tapeworms, and typhoid fever. Your medical officers will discuss specific standards for water and food preparation in Botswana during pre-service training.

Abstinence is the only certain choice for preventing infection with HIV and other sexually transmitted diseases. You are taking risks if you choose to be sexually active. To lessen risk, use a condom every time you have sex. Whether your partner is a host country citizen, a fellow Volunteer, or anyone else, do not assume this person is free of HIV/AIDS or other STDs. You will receive more information from the medical officers about this important issue.

Volunteers are expected to adhere to an effective means of birth control to prevent an unplanned pregnancy. Your medical officers can help you decide on the most appropriate method to suit your individual needs. Contraceptive methods are available without charge from the medical office.

It is critical to your health that you promptly report to the medical office or other designated facility for scheduled immunizations, and that you let the medical officers know immediately of significant illnesses and injuries.

Women's Health Information

Pregnancy is treated in the same manner as other Volunteer health conditions that require medical attention but also have programmatic ramifications. The Peace Corps is responsible for determining the medical risk and the availability of appropriate medical care if the Volunteer remains in-country. Given the circumstances under which Volunteers live and work in Peace Corps countries, it is rare that the Peace Corps' medical and programmatic standards for continued service during pregnancy can be met.

If feminine hygiene products are not available for you to purchase on the local market, the Peace Corps medical officers in Botswana will provide them. If you require a specific product, please bring a three-month supply with you.

Your Peace Corps Medical Kit

The Peace Corps medical officers will provide you with a kit that contains basic items necessary to prevent and treat illnesses that may occur during service. Kit items can be periodically restocked at the medical office.

Medical Kit Contents
Ace bandages

Adhesive tape

American Red Cross First Aid & Safety Handbook

Antacid tablets (Tums)

Antibiotic ointment (Bacitracin/Neomycin/Polymycin B)

Antiseptic antimicrobial skin cleaner (Hibiclens)

Band-Aids

Butterfly closures

Calamine lotion

Cepacol lozenges

Condoms

Dental floss

Diphenhydramine HCL 25 mg (Benadryl)

Insect repellent stick (Cutter)

Iodine tablets (for water purification)

Lip balm (Chapstick)

Oral rehydration salts

Oral thermometer (Fahrenheit)

Pseudoephedrine HCL 30 mg (Sudafed)

Robitussin-DM lozenges (for cough)

Scissors

Sterile gauze pads

Tetrahydrozaline eyedrops (Visine)

Tinactin (antifungal cream)

Tweezers

Before You Leave: A Medical Checklist

If there has been any change in your health—physical, mental, or dental—since you submitted your examination reports to the Peace Corps, you must immediately notify the Office of Medical Services. Failure to disclose new illnesses, injuries, allergies, or pregnancy can endanger your health and may jeopardize your eligibility to serve.

If your dental exam was done more than a year ago, or if your physical exam is more than two years old, contact the Office of Medical Services to find out whether you need to update your records. If your dentist or Peace Corps dental consultant has recommended that you undergo dental treatment or repair, you must complete that work and make sure your dentist sends requested confirmation reports or X-rays to the Office of Medical Services.

If you wish to avoid having duplicate vaccinations, contact your physician's office to obtain a copy of your immunization record and bring it to your pre-departure orientation. If you have any immunizations prior to Peace Corps service, the Peace Corps cannot reimburse you for the cost. The Peace Corps will provide all the immunizations necessary for your overseas assignment, either at your pre-departure orientation or shortly after you arrive in Botswana. You do not need to begin taking malaria medication prior to departure.

Bring a three-month supply of any prescription or over-the-counter medication you use on a regular basis, including birth control pills. Although the Peace Corps cannot reimburse you for this three-month supply, it will order refills during your service. While awaiting shipment—which can take several months—you will be dependent on your own medication supply. The Peace Corps will not pay for herbal or nonprescribed medications, such as St. John's wort, glucosamine, selenium, or antioxidant supplements.

You are encouraged to bring copies of medical prescriptions signed by your physician. This is not a requirement, but they might come in handy if you are questioned in transit about carrying a three-month supply of prescription drugs.

If you wear eyeglasses, bring two pairs with you—a pair and a spare. If a pair breaks, the Peace Corps will replace them, using the information your doctor in the United States provided on the eyeglasses form during your examination. The Peace Corps discourages you from using contact lenses during your service to reduce your risk of developing a serious infection or other eye disease. Most Peace Corps countries do not have appropriate water and sanitation to support eye care with the use of contact lenses. The Peace Corps will not supply or replace contact lenses or associated solutions unless an ophthalmologist has recommended their use for a specific medical condition and the Peace Corps' Office of Medical Services has given approval.

If you are eligible for Medicare, are over 50 years of age, or have a health condition that may restrict your future participation in health care plans, you may wish to consult an insurance specialist about unique coverage needs before your departure. The Peace Corps will provide all necessary health care from the time you leave for your pre-departure orientation until you complete your service. When you finish, you will be entitled to the post-service health care benefits described in the Peace Corps Volunteer Handbook. You may wish to consider keeping an existing health plan in effect during your service if you think age or pre-existing conditions might prevent you from re-enrolling in your current plan when you return home.

Safety and Security—Our Partnership

Serving as a Volunteer overseas entails certain safety and security risks. Living and traveling in an unfamiliar environment, a limited understanding of the local language and culture, and the perception of being a wealthy American are some of the factors that can put a Volunteer at risk. Property theft and burglaries are not uncommon. Incidents of physical and sexual assault do occur, although almost all Volunteers complete their two years of service without serious personal safety problems.

Beyond knowing that Peace Corps approaches safety and security as a partnership with you, it might be helpful to see how this partnership works. Peace Corps has policies, procedures, and training in place to promote your safety. We depend on you to follow those policies and to put into practice what you have learned. An example of how this works in practice—in this case to help manage the risk of burglary—is:

- Peace Corps assesses the security environment where you will live and work

- Peace Corps inspects the house where you will live according to established security criteria

- Peace Corps provides you with resources to take measures such as installing new locks

- Peace Corps ensures you are welcomed by host country authorities in your new community

- Peace Corps responds to security concerns that you raise

- You lock your doors and windows

- You adopt a lifestyle appropriate to the community where you live

- You get to know neighbors

- You decide if purchasing personal articles insurance is appropriate for you

- You don't change residences before being authorized by Peace Corps

- You communicate concerns that you have to Peace Corps staff

Factors that Contribute to Volunteer Risk

There are several factors that can heighten a Volunteer's risk, many of which are within the Volunteer's control. By far the most common crime that Volunteers experience is theft. Thefts often occur when Volunteers are away from their sites, in crowded locations (such as markets or on public transportation), and when leaving items unattended.

Before you depart for Botswana there are several measures you can take to reduce your risk:

- Leave valuable objects in the U.S.

- Leave copies of important documents and account numbers with someone you trust in the U.S.

- Purchase a hidden money pouch or "dummy" wallet as a decoy

- Purchase personal articles insurance

After you arrive in Botswana, you will receive more detailed information about common crimes, factors that contribute to Volunteer risk, and local strategies to reduce that risk. For example, Volunteers in Botswana learn to:

- Choose safe routes and times for travel, and travel with someone trusted by the community whenever possible

- Make sure one's personal appearance is respectful of local customs

- Avoid high-crime areas

- Know the local language to get help in an emergency

- Make friends with local people who are respected in the community

- Limit alcohol consumption

As you can see from this list, you must be willing to work hard and adapt your lifestyle to minimize the potential for being a target for crime. As with anywhere in the world, crime does exist in Botswana. You can reduce your risk by avoiding situations that place you at risk and by taking precautions. Crime at the village or town level is less frequent than in the large cities; people know each other and generally are less likely to steal from their neighbors. Tourist attractions in large towns are favorite worksites for pickpockets.

Houses and rooms left empty during holidays also create tempting opportunities. Wherever you are in Botswana, alcohol can fuel unsafe driving, unsafe sex, and sexual assaults. In general, individuals are easier targets than groups and women are easier targets than men. While being aware of these matters may seem like common sense, our altruism often overrides common sense until something bad happens. While whistles and exclamations may be fairly common on the street, this behavior can be reduced if you dress conservatively, abide by local cultural norms, and respond according to the training you will receive.

Staying Safe: Don't Be a Target for Crime

You must be prepared to take on a large degree of responsibility for your own safety. You can make yourself less of a target, ensure that your home is secure, and develop relationships in your community that will make you an unlikely victim of crime. While the factors that contribute to your risk in Botswana may be different, in many ways you can do what you would do if you moved to a new city anywhere: Be cautious, check things out, ask questions, learn about your neighborhood, know where the more risky locations are, use common sense, and be aware. You can reduce your vulnerability to crime by integrating into your community, learning the local language, acting responsibly, and abiding by Peace Corps policies and procedures. Serving safely and effectively in Botswana will require that you accept some restrictions on your current lifestyle.

Support from Staff

If a trainee or Volunteer is the victim of a safety incident, Peace Corps staff is prepared to provide support. All Peace Corps posts have procedures in place to respond to incidents of crime committed against Volunteers. The first priority for all posts in the aftermath of an incident is to ensure the Volunteer is safe and receiving medical treatment as needed. After assuring the safety of the Volunteer, Peace Corps staff response may include reassessing the Volunteer's worksite and housing arrangements and making any adjustments, as needed. In some cases, the nature of the incident may necessitate a site or housing transfer. Peace Corps staff will also assist Volunteers with preserving their rights to pursue legal sanctions against the perpetrators of the crime. It is very important that Volunteers report incidents as they occur, not only to protect their peer Volunteers, but also to preserve the future right to prosecute. Should Volunteers decide later in the process that they want to proceed with the prosecution of their assailant, this option may no longer exist if the evidence of the event has not been preserved at the time of the incident.

Crime Data for Botswana

Crime data and statistics for Botswana, which are updated yearly, are available at the following link: http://www.peacecorps.gov/countrydata/botswana

Please take the time to review this important information.

Few Peace Corps Volunteers are victims of serious crimes, and crimes that do occur overseas are investigated and prosecuted by local authorities through the local courts system. If you are the victim of a crime, you will decide if you wish to pursue prosecution. If you decide to prosecute, Peace Corps will be there to assist you. One of our tasks is to ensure you are fully informed of your options and understand how the local legal process works. Peace Corps will help you ensure your rights are protected to the fullest extent possible under the laws of the country.

If you are the victim of a serious crime, you will learn how to get to a safe location as quickly as possible and contact your Peace Corps office. It's important that you notify Peace Corps as soon as you can so Peace Corps can provide you with the help you need.

Volunteer Safety Support in Botswana

The Peace Corps' approach to safety is a five-pronged plan to help you stay safe during your service and includes the following: information sharing, Volunteer training, site selection criteria, a detailed emergency action plan, and protocols for addressing safety and security incidents. Botswana's in-country safety program is outlined below.

The Peace Corps/Botswana office will keep you informed of any issues that may impact Volunteer safety through **information sharing**. Regular updates will be provided in Volunteer newsletters and in memorandums from the country director. In the event of a critical situation or emergency, you will be contacted through the emergency communication network. An important component of the capacity of Peace Corps to keep you informed is your buy-in to the partnership concept with the Peace Corps staff. It is expected that you will do your part in ensuring that Peace Corps staff members are kept apprised of your movements in-country so they are able to inform you.

Volunteer training will include sessions on specific safety and security issues in Botswana. This training will prepare you to adopt a culturally appropriate lifestyle and exercise judgment that promotes safety and reduces risk in your home, at work, and while traveling. Safety training is offered throughout service and is integrated into the language, cross-cultural aspects, health, and other components of training. You will be expected to successfully complete all training competencies in a variety of areas, including safety and security, as a condition of service.

Certain **site selection criteria** are used to determine safe housing for Volunteers before their arrival. The Peace Corps staff works closely with host communities and counterpart agencies to help prepare them for a Volunteer's arrival and to establish expectations of their respective roles in supporting the Volunteer. Each site is inspected before the Volunteer's arrival to ensure placement in appropriate, safe, and secure housing and worksites. Site selection is based, in part, on any relevant site history; access to medical, banking, postal, and other essential services; availability of communications, transportation, and markets; different housing options and living arrangements; and other Volunteer support needs.

You will also learn about Peace Corps/Botswana's **detailed emergency action plan,** which is implemented in the event of civil or political unrest or a natural disaster. When you arrive at your site, you will complete and submit a site locator form with your address, contact information, and a map to your house. If there is a security threat, you will gather with other Volunteers in Botswana at predetermined locations until the situation is resolved or the Peace Corps decides to evacuate.

Finally, in order for the Peace Corps to be fully responsive to the needs of Volunteers, it is imperative that Volunteers immediately report any security incident to the Peace Corps office. The Peace Corps has established **protocols for addressing safety and security incidents** in a timely and appropriate manner, and it collects and evaluates safety and security data to track trends and develop strategies to minimize risks to future Volunteers.

DIVERSITY AND
CROSS-CULTURAL ISSUES

In fulfilling its mandate to share the face of America with host countries, the Peace Corps is making special efforts to assure that all of America's richness is reflected in the Volunteer corps. More Americans of color are serving in today's Peace Corps than at any time in recent history. Differences in race, ethnic background, age, religion, and sexual orientation are expected and welcomed among our Volunteers. Part of the Peace Corps' mission is to help dispel any notion that Americans are all of one origin or race and to establish that each of us is as thoroughly American as the other despite our many differences.

Our diversity helps us accomplish that goal. In other ways, however, it poses challenges. In Botswana, as in other Peace Corps host countries, Volunteers' behavior, lifestyle, background, and beliefs are judged in a cultural context very different from their own. Certain personal perspectives or characteristics commonly accepted in the United States may be quite uncommon, unacceptable, or even repressed in Botswana.

Outside of Botswana's capital, residents of rural communities have had relatively little direct exposure to other cultures, races, religions, and lifestyles. What people view as typical American behavior or norms may be a misconception, such as the belief that all Americans are rich and have blond hair and blue eyes. The people of Botswana are justly known for their generous hospitality to foreigners; however, members of the community in which you will live may display a range of reactions to cultural differences that you present.

To ease the transition and adapt to life in Botswana, you may need to make some temporary, yet fundamental compromises in how you present yourself as an American and as an individual. For example, female trainees and Volunteers may not be able to exercise the independence available to them in the United States; political discussions need to be handled with great care; and some of your personal beliefs may best remain undisclosed. You will need to develop techniques and personal strategies for coping with these and other limitations. The Peace Corps staff will lead diversity and sensitivity discussions during pre-service training and will be on call to provide support, but the challenge ultimately will be your own.

Overview of Diversity in Botswana

The Peace Corps staff in Botswana recognizes the adjustment issues that come with diversity and will endeavor to provide support and guidance. During pre-service training, several sessions will be held to discuss diversity and coping mechanisms. We look forward to having male and female Volunteers from a variety of races, ethnic groups, ages, religions, and sexual orientations, and hope that you will become part of a diverse group of Americans who take pride in supporting one another and demonstrating the richness of American culture.

What Might a Volunteer Face?

Possible Issues for Female Volunteers

To address restrictive laws and traditions of its society, Botswana has a constitution that protects women's rights. The country has made great strides in gender equity in the modern sector. Ministerial, senior-level government, and private-sector posts are held by women. In addition, the government has developed a national gender program to improve the lives of vulnerable women. Nevertheless, rural, less educated women at the lower end of the socioeconomic scale tend to have less authority and responsibility than men do for income, spending, and reproductive health. Although this is changing, many rural communities have not had much experience with women who take on professional roles, remain unmarried, and live away from their families. Thus, female Volunteers may experience a great deal of unwanted attention and may need to practice discretion in public. During both cross-cultural and safety training sessions, all Volunteers are provided with strategies and practice in limiting and responding to unwanted attention. Also, younger female Volunteers may find it takes longer to establish credibility with co-workers than male or older Volunteers.

Possible Issues for Volunteers of Color

Most Batswana in cities and towns are aware of the different racial and ethnic groups that exist in the United States. However, this level of knowledge and understanding greatly diminishes among rural populations. African-American Volunteers may not be recognized as Americans. They may be expected to learn local languages more quickly than other Volunteers, may or may not be accepted more readily into the culture than other Volunteers, and may be treated according to local social norms because they are assumed to be African.

Hispanic-American and Asian-American Volunteers may also be perceived as not being American. Batswana may expect Asian Americans to exhibit stereotyped behavior observed in films, sometimes referred to as the "kung fu syndrome." Asian Americans are often assumed to be Chinese. In addition, the presence of Asian merchants in the country may have an impact on how Asian-American Volunteers are perceived.

Possible Issues for Senior Volunteers

In Botswana, older members of society are viewed and treated with a great deal of respect. Issues for older Volunteers are more likely to be in relation to their younger fellow Volunteers. Older Volunteers may meet individuals in the Peace Corps community who have little understanding of, or respect for, the lives and experiences of senior Americans and may not be able to offer the necessary personal support. Older Volunteers, in turn, may be inclined to withdraw from full participation in order to "give the younger folks their turn," and may be reluctant to share personal, sexual, or health concerns. They may not find appropriate role models among the Peace Corps staff or may find that younger Volunteers look to them for more advice than they feel comfortable giving. Finally, older Volunteers may need to be assertive about asking for an effective individual approach to language learning during pre-service training.

Possible Issues for Married Couple Volunteers

In Botswana, public displays of affection between married couples is not a common occurrence and may be considered as showing a poor example for the younger generation. Kissing and affectionate touching is confined to the bedroom. At the same time, you might see Batswana friends holding hands in public – two women, two men, or man and a woman.

Possible Issues for Gay, Lesbian, or Bisexual Volunteers

In general, Batswana view homosexuality as immoral; it is illegal according to the country's constitution. Homosexuality certainly exists in Botswana, but not with the same level of acceptance as in the United States. Because of cultural norms, homosexual Volunteers may discover that they cannot be open about their sexual orientation and have to serve for two years without revealing to their community that they are gay. This omission might lead to a lessened intensity or depth to friendships formed, particularly those with community members, which could be disheartening. Homosexual or bisexual Volunteers may also serve for two years without meeting another homosexual or bisexual Volunteer, although Peace Corps/Botswana has an internal support network to deal with Volunteer issues of diversity and peer support. Lesbians, like all American women, are likely to have to deal with constant questions about boyfriends, marriage, and sex, while gay men may have to deal with machismo: talk of sexual conquests, girl watching, and dirty jokes.

A recommended resource for support and advice prior to and during your service is the Lesbian, Gay, Bisexual & Transgender U.S. Peace Corps Alumni website at www.lgbrpcv.org .

Possible Religious Issues for Volunteers

Most Batswana have some religious affiliation, and many attend church regularly. Most meetings, government-sponsored or not, often start with a prayer. Both Christian and non-Christian Volunteers may be expected to attend church with the members of their community. They may be asked to explain why they do not belong to a certain Christian denomination or may be actively recruited by a Christian group. Volunteers may not be able to adequately convey their own religious beliefs because of language or cultural barriers.

Possible Issues for Volunteers With Disabilities
As part of the medical clearance process, the Peace Corps Office of Medical Services determined that you were physically and emotionally capable, with or without reasonable accommodations, to perform a full tour of Volunteer service in Country X without unreasonable risk of harm to yourself or interruption of service. The Peace Corps/ Country X staff will work with disabled Volunteers to make reasonable accommodations for them in training, housing, jobsites, or other areas to enable them to serve safely and effectively.

FREQUENTLY ASKED QUESTIONS

How much luggage am I allowed to bring to Botswana?

Most airlines have baggage size and weight limits and assess charges for transport of baggage that exceeds those limits. The Peace Corps has its own size and weight limits and will not pay the cost of transport for baggage that exceeds these limits. The Peace Corps' allowance is two checked pieces of luggage with combined dimensions of both pieces not to exceed 107 inches (length + width + height) and a carry-on bag with dimensions of no more than 45 inches. Checked baggage should not exceed 100 pounds total with a maximum weight of 50 pounds for any one bag.

Peace Corps Volunteers are not allowed to take pets, weapons, explosives, radio transmitters (shortwave radios are permitted), automobiles, or motorcycles to their overseas assignments. Do not pack flammable materials or liquids such as lighter fluid, cleaning solvents, hair spray, or aerosol containers. This is an important safety precaution.

What is the electric current in Botswana?

It is 220 volts, 50 hertz. Plugs/outlets consist of both three-prong round and three-prong square shapes. It is recommended that you buy a universal adapter from the US, but you can find adapters of lesser quality in Botswana.

How much money should I bring?

Volunteers are expected to live at the same level as the people in their community. You will be given a walk-around allowance during Pre-Service Training, a settling-in allowance once you swear in, and a monthly living allowance during service, all of which should cover your expenses. Volunteers often wish to bring additional money for vacation travel to other countries. Credit cards are preferable to cash; traveler's checks are only rarely used anymore in this region. If you choose to bring extra money, bring the amount that will suit your own travel plans and needs. Remember that if cash is lost, you will not be reimbursed by any property insurance.

When can I take vacation and have people visit me?

Each Volunteer accrues two vacation days per month of service (excluding training). Leave may not be taken during training, the first three months of service, or the last three months of service, except in conjunction with an authorized emergency leave. Family and friends are welcome to visit you after pre-service training and the first three months of service as long as their stay does not interfere with your work – and remember, the PCV cannot travel out of site on vacation. Extended visitors at your site are not encouraged and may require permission from your Country Director. The Peace Corps is not able to provide your visitors with visa, medical, or travel assistance.

Will my belongings be covered by insurance?

The Peace Corps does not provide insurance coverage for personal effects; Volunteers are ultimately responsible for the safekeeping of their personal belongings. However, you can purchase personal property insurance before you leave. If you wish, you may contact your own insurance company; additionally, insurance application forms will be provided, and we encourage you to consider them carefully. Volunteers should not ship or take valuable items overseas. Jewelry, watches, radios, cameras, and expensive appliances are subject to loss, theft, and breakage, and in many places, satisfactory maintenance and repair services are not available. Most Volunteers in Botswana agree that personal property insurance is worth the cost.

Do I need an international driver's license?

Volunteers in Botswana do not need an international driver's license, because they are prohibited from operating privately owned motorized vehicles. Most urban travel is by bus or taxi. Rural travel ranges from buses and minibuses to trucks, bicycles, and lots of walking. On very rare occasions, a Volunteer may be asked to drive a sponsor's vehicle, but this can occur only with prior written permission from the Country Director. Should this occur, the Volunteer may obtain a local driver's license. A US driver's license will facilitate the process, so bring it with you just in case. You may also wish to rent a car when you are on leave on travel outside of the country.

What should I bring as gifts for Batswana friends and my host family?

This is not a requirement. A token of friendship is sufficient. Some gift suggestions include knickknacks for the house; pictures, books, or calendars of American scenes; souvenirs from your area; hard candies that will not melt or spoil; or photos to give away.

Where will my site assignment be when I finish training and how isolated will I be?

Peace Corps trainees are not assigned to individual sites until after they have completed pre-service training. This gives Peace Corps staff the opportunity to assess each trainee's technical and language skills prior to assigning sites, in addition to finalizing site selections with their ministry counterparts. If feasible, you may have the opportunity to provide input on your site preferences, including geographical location, distance from other Volunteers, and living conditions. However, keep in mind that many factors influence the site selection process and that the Peace Corps cannot guarantee placement where you would ideally like to be. Most Volunteers in Botswana live in small towns or in rural villages and are usually within one hour from another Volunteer.

How can my family contact me in an emergency?

The Peace Corps' Counseling and Outreach Unit (COU) provides assistance in handling emergencies affecting trainees and Volunteers or their families. Before leaving the United States, instruct your family to notify the Counseling and Outreach Unit immediately if an emergency arises, such as a serious illness or death of a family member. During normal business hours, the number for the Counseling and Outreach Unit is 855.855.1961, then select option 2; or directly at 202-692-1470. After normal business hours and on weekends and holidays, the COU duty officer can be reached at the above number. For non-emergency questions, your family can get information from your country desk staff at the Peace Corps by calling 855.855.1961.

Can I call home from Botswana?

Yes. Volunteers receive a cellphone during training. Volunteers often text or call home and ask to be called back or pre-arrange a time to be called on their cellphone or on a private or office phone.

Should I bring a cellular phone with me?

While cellular phone services are widely available in Botswana, it is not advisable to bring a cellphone from the United States unless you check with the manufacturer and confirm that the phone will work in Botswana. In all cases, these phones are the type with SIM cards that can be changed in and out. Smart phones work and are available in Botswana, although they are quite expensive. If you choose to bring a smart phone from home, be sure to unlock it for use prior to leaving the U.S. SIM cards in Botswana cost about $3. The cost of a new basic cellphone in Botswana is approximately $30.

Will there be email and Internet access?
Should I bring my computer?

Internet service is widely available in Botswana; most larger villages and towns have internet cafes. Wireless internet is becoming increasingly common, particularly in the cities. Additionally, Internet is available via most major cellphone networks.

The choice about whether to bring a computer is an individual one. The Peace Corps does not require Volunteers to bring a computer. Not all Volunteers live at sites with electricity and the climate in Botswana can be tough on sensitive electronics. In addition, peripherals like printer cartridges and disks are very expensive locally. Yet, Peace Corps quarterly report forms are submitted electronically. If you do not have your own computer you can arrange to complete the form at Internet cafes or possibly neighboring Volunteers' sites. The Peace Corps sometimes communicates with Volunteers via email; however, the Peace Corps keeps an updated list of which Volunteers do not have consistent Internet access and will communicate with these Volunteers via phone, text message, or post.

Despite the difficulties, most current Volunteers recommend that you bring a laptop citing it as a useful tool for both work and entertainment. If you bring a computer or other valuable equipment you should consider purchasing personal property insurance AND ensure that you have antiviral software good for the length of your service. Computer viruses and worms are rampant throughout the country. Bring antiviral software hard discs with you that will cover the length of your service. Downloading anti-viral software by internet is not always possible due to slow Internet connections.

What about credit cards?

If you bring credit cards, make sure they are good for the length of your service. Renewing cards can be a challenge from Botswana. You should also talk to your bank to unlock your card for use in Botswana and find out the procedure for informing your bank when you travel to neighboring countries. Otherwise, your card is likely to be frozen after one use.

WELCOME LETTERS FROM BOTSWANA VOLUNTEERS

Greetings Bots Invitees!

I welcome your consideration to serve in one of the four program areas confronting HIV/AIDS in Botswana.

You are being offered an opportunity and a privilege to be part of a new culture while facing many challenges in adjustment and role definition. My experiences have allowed me to be an observer, learner, and a participant in events rich in culture and the realities of daily life for many Batswana. Additionally, I am now bonded for life with over 50 incredible individuals who make up Bots 8.

In a recent discussion with several of my PCV colleagues we concluded that until you are in your role, you are unable to conceive the complete reality of serving. However, there are many ways of preparing yourself, as recommended by the Peace Corps. I followed their recommendations and found them very helpful.

Once you receive your invitation packet, you are faced with your most significant decision, whether or not to accept. I strongly suggest that you read the material carefully and weigh it honestly and openly against your understanding of yourself. Perhaps having an objective person or counselor also read the material and offer feedback would be helpful. Occasionally we were surprised by a trainee's reaction to something that was clearly spelled out in the invitation packet.

In terms of clothing, having wrinkle resistant fabrics that can withstand hand washing with harsh soap is the goal. The soil is reddish so keep that in mind when choosing white clothing, although bleach is available. Shoes get beat up quickly walking on dirt paths with rocks, even with the Merrills I brought. The bottom line is that Batswana do not wear wrinkled clothing or dirty shoes so keep that in mind when you are selecting items to bring. For those of us in office settings, the attire is professional and most of the women wear high heels.

As an older Volunteer, I will offer a few comments on stamina and physical fitness. Although the Peace Corps does not have fitness requirements, perhaps that will be a consideration in the future with people serving in their 70s and 80s. Accommodations are made for medical necessity, but not for age or fitness level. As a result, all ages have physical demands. For example, to access food and banking, I walk an hour and ride a bus for two hours per round trip. Everything is carried either in a backpack or other bag for traveling, groceries, or books. I lug large pails of water for bathing and laundry and do extensive walking in my role as a Volunteer for district AIDS coordination. Therefore, if your lifestyle has been sedentary of late, I would suggest a regular program of fitness to prepare you for a life on foot with heavy packages. You will appreciate the effort made to ease your transition to living in a village without a car.

I wish you the very best while deliberating this life changing and exciting decision!

Sincerely,
Karen "Rebaone" Butler, Bots 8
Goodhope District AIDS Coordination

Welcome to Peace Corps Botswana!

As you are preparing to leave the USA for Botswana I am sure you have a million questions running though your head; what will the food be like? What will the culture be like? Did I pack enough underwear? While all of these thoughts are normal and it is difficult to put them out of your mind, I urge you to enjoy the adventure and rest assured that you will find everything you need when you arrive.

When you arrive the questions won't subside, they will multiply. This is the exciting part about learning about a new culture and place, embrace it. There will be many questions that will arise during training that won't really be able to be answered until you get your site and final assignment.

As you are thinking about packing worry less about clothing. The things you will long for are the items that remind you of home. If you have something you can't live without in the US, you will probably want it with you in Botswana too. Half of the things I packed, I turned out not needing. The things that I have found most helpful during my service; good pots and pans, spices, coffee and a French press, good walking and running shoes and my iPhone. Electronics are a large part of our daily life in America and sometimes the change of 'unplugging' is difficult. You could be in a village with no electricity or you could be in a city.

Either way, keep this is mind; what do you enjoy doing in your free time in America? Often time's volunteers find that they enjoy watching movies or tv shows, it can be a good way to decompress after a long day, share a bit of American culture, have a laugh or remind you of home. The external hard drive that I packed has been my saving grace some days, especially if I am sick, missing family or just having an off day. I am quite an avid reader but sometimes it's comforting to just watch a movie.

If you want to stay connected on the internet, keep in mind that your access to wi-fi is generally non-existent unless you are in a major city, I mention this because many volunteers with ipads have difficulty ever accessing the internet with them. You will be able to figure out a way to access the internet, even if you are in one of the most remote corners of Botswana.

While the packing might be the thing at the forefront of your mind at the moment take time to begin learning Setswana. The more you learn before you arrive the better off you will be. There are many people throughout Botswana that speak English but you will instantly gain respect and trust in your site if you can carry out a decent conversation in Setswana. Don't be afraid to make mistakes either, throw in English words if you don't know something, you might get a laugh but you will probably also make a friend.

Use the rest of your time to do the things you enjoy in America and spend as much time as possible with family and friends. It is a great journey and I guaranty you will learn a lot about yourself and the world if you are patient, persistent and kind. Be open to new experiences and enjoy the ride!

Rachel 'Kesego' Ecklund, Bots 11
PCV Botswana 2011-2013
School and Community Liaison for Life Skills
Morwamosu, Botswana

Greetings Bots Invitees!

Welcome to the Peace Corps and welcome to an experience of a lifetime and one that you will never regret!

Perhaps a lot of questions are running through your mind? Perhaps you are a little nervous about such a commitment, especially without knowing "exactly" what you will be doing. Congratulations, you're normal!

I can tell you that you will receive excellent training here before you set out to your location within the country. I can also tell you that you have access to excellent support in the Peace Corps staff as well as the support of many of the other new Peace Corps Volunteers you will have bonded with during your weeks of training. Last, but not least, there is the support from other Peace Corps Volunteers already serving within the country. Yes, you have a new family here...and for life!

The important thing you need to have is something you have read over and over, but so incredibly important so I will emphasize it yet again...and make sure you pack this when you come....a positive attitude! Pack some fortitude too. Why? Well things here are not the same as in the USA. In the US you have your ups and downs in life and you will here too. But in the US you have some experience in handling these situations. Here you are open to a whole new world. Maybe you will lose electric power and/or water for some hours each week... You will learn how to deal with these situations and they will become just another part of the adjustment.

The Sub-Saharan culture is unlike any culture I had previously experienced and it will take some time to get used to. Also, things happen very slowly here. Did I mention that things happen very slowly here? You will eventually see some aspects of "African time" that are nice for a change.

Bring clothes that will stand up to hand washing….and yes, you will be doing the washing. Perma-press clothes and quick drying socks and underwear will be very good investments. Buy a pair of shoes that are high quality….you will not regret spending the extra money as they take a beating here.

If you would like to stay in shape…Botswana is for you as you will be walking, walking and walking. I am an older volunteer and I love the walking. You will meet villagers and children along the way and they all will remember your name…remembering all their names is not so easy.

It will take some time to get used to your location but you will eventually find something to do for community activity (your niche!) that will be both beneficial to your community and to your sense of being a valuable member of it.

My opinion - a laptop is a must. Even if no access to internet in your village there will be places you will have access. You can communicate with family/friends, helpful to your work and also for doing research on various subjects that you know little about but someone needs that information and you are deemed an "expert" by the mere fact you are Peace Corps. Lastly, a laptop affords you access to movies which are good form of relaxation. Also a good separate hard drive for all the movies and music you will share with your fellow PCVs.

Okay…time to strap yourself in…and get ready for the ride of your life!

Sincerely,
David "Kabelo" LaFratta, Bots 12
Gumare - District AIDS Coordination

Welcome to Peace Corps Botswana!

You're in for an adventure of a lifetime. While the Peace Corps is completely different for each person, I can assure you that two years in the Peace Corps will challenge, excite, motivate, and inspire each person that approaches the experience with an open heart.

You've been blessed to receive an invitation to an extraordinarily unique African country. You'll hear people say that Botswana is "the gem of Africa", and although it sounds a little cliché, I can't help but agree. You'll fall in love with the people, the culture, the peaceful environment, and breathtaking scenery. Botswana is a truly remarkable country to be serving in.

Keep in mind how challenging development work can be (especially in terms of behavior change) to help regulate your expectations. While you may not see direct results of your blood, sweat, and tears during service, rest assured that you will make an impact. Our work to fight against HIV is powerful and worthwhile. The lessons we teach others will stay with them for the rest of their lives. You simply can't put a price on education and empowerment. It's an investment worth making.

You have so much to look forward to during your service, but for now, spend more time with your loved ones than you do worrying about packing. Soak up all the things you love in the states… family, friends, pets, outdoor activities, hobbies, etc. Don't spend your last few weeks stressing out about packing. Bring things that are important to YOU, whatever will make you feel more like who you were back at home. You are still the same YOU during service. Pack that yoga mat, carry on that guitar, and shove in your teddy bear last minute. And most importantly, be sure you bring your best attitude, sense of humor, plenty of flexibility, and desire for adventure.

Joining the Peace Corps is a decision you won't regret.

Cheers,
Tate Van Winkle, Bots 12
Clinic & Health Team Volunteer
Kang, Botswana

WHAT TO PACK

This list has been compiled by Volunteers serving in Botswana and is based on their experience. Use it as an informal guide in making your own list, bearing in mind that each experience is individual. There is no perfect list! You obviously cannot bring everything on the list, so consider those items that make the most sense to you personally and professionally. You can always have things sent to you later. As you decide what to bring, keep in mind that you have an 100-pound weight limit on baggage. And remember, you can get almost everything you need in Botswana.

Note that while the climate is comfortable most of the year, houses do not have heat, making the winters MUCH colder than you might expect, and Volunteers do wear layers, long underwear at night, etc. Much of Botswana can be dusty and sandy; many Volunteers bring durable clothes that are easy to clean. You will likely be washing your clothes by hand.

Expectations for your dress are also determined by your job placement. Anyone working in a government office (all but NGO Volunteers) will work with colleagues who must comply with government guidelines dated March 19, 2009:

Interpretation of General Order 34.1 on Dress While on Duty

Addressees are reminded that it is mandatory for public employees to dress in a manner that reflects credit on the Public Service, in line with General Order 34.1.

In order to ensure consistency in the application of General Order 34.1, dress indicated below shall not be worn while on duty.
a. clothing that reveals cleavage, bareback, chest, armpits, stomach and underwear
b. torn, dirty, wrinkled, or frayed clothing
c. casual and gym wear, including jeans and shorts
d. short and/or tight skirts, pants and dresses.
e. body hugging clothes
f. tops, shirts, and T-shirts with offensive words, logo, pictures, cartoons, or slogans
g. casual and sports shoes
h. hats and caps (However, religious and traditional head covers and headgears may be allowed at the discretion of the permanent secretary.)
i. colorful hairstyles

General Clothing

For Men

- Dress slacks and khaki trousers (jeans are not appropriate at work)
- Lightweight cotton dress shirts (T-shirts are not appropriate at work)
- Dress shoes or loafers (tennis shoes or sandals are not appropriate at work)
- Sports coat or suit for special events (even more important than a tie for some events)
- Ties; if you are in the Life Skills program, male teachers do wear ties daily
- Durable jeans (for weekends, travel, or after-work wear)
- Shorts (to wear in your home)
- Bathing suit
- Casual shoes (tennis shoes, running shoes, sandals, etc.)
- Warm coat (can buy in Botswana but not always of the same quality)
- Sweaters or fleece pullovers
- Thermal underwear
- A few pairs of thick socks
- Gloves or mittens
- Lightweight raincoat or poncho

For Women

- Dresses or skirts (knee-length or longer for work, no denim; nice slacks are acceptable in some settings)
- Lightweight cotton blouses
- Dress shoes (for work, make sure they are easy to walk in)
- Durable jeans (for weekends, travel, or after-work wear)
- Long shorts
- Bathing suit
- Casual shoes (tennis shoes, running shoes, sandals, etc.)
- Warm coat (can buy in Botswana but not always of the same quality)
- Sweaters or fleece pullovers
- Cotton leggings (can be very useful in winter under skirts and pants)
- A few pairs of thick socks
- Gloves or mittens
- Lightweight raincoat or poncho
- Sports bra, yoga pants, other exercise/leisure clothing

Shoes

Women's shoes larger than size 10 and smaller than a size 7 may be difficult to find. Most other types of shoes are readily available in Botswana, although they may not be of the same quality found in the United States. Casual shoes should be especially durable–sand, gravel, and lots of walking tend to be hard on casual flip-flops. (Teva/Chacos are better.) Good running shoes are hard to find and are expensive.

Personal Hygiene and Toiletry Items

All basic toiletry items are available in Botswana, so you only need to bring enough for the first five or six weeks. Although the selection here may not be what you are used to, the quality is generally quite good. Medicine and first aid items will be available from the Peace Corps Medical Office once you are sworn in as a Volunteer.

Miscellaneous

- Headlamp (good for reading at night if lamps are dim or far away, finding outdoor latrine at night, load shedding, etc.)
- French press (if you appreciate good coffee)
- Leatherman/Swiss Army Knife – will come in handy for camping, maintenance
- Good sunglasses, a hat (or two) and umbrella (There are about 345 sunny days per year in Botswana; the Peace Corps will supply sunscreen, although some people prefer a specific type for their face. The umbrella comes in

handy for blocking the sun. You may also easily purchase cheap umbrellas, hats, and not-so-good sunglasses in shopping villages)
- Three-month supply of any prescription medicine you take
- Electronics—cameras, MP3 players, external hard drives, etc. are available in Botswana but are very expensive (AA and D batteries are the most commonly available size) *note: take serial numbers/get insurance for all electronics in case of theft. Police will use serial numbers to find them.*
- Sleeping bag (for warmth during winter, traveling, staying at friends' houses – rectangular is preferable to also use as a blanket at home)
- Cooking spices, such as basil, cilantro, taco seasoning, and more rare spices (available in Gaborone, but not up-country)
- Things to entertain yourself or others who visit (varies by Volunteer, but may include games (cards, Scrabble), books, and knitting supplies)
- Maps, postcards from your hometown, pictures of family, mementos (great for decorating your new home and for telling people where you are from)
- Stationery, envelopes, good pens (expensive and difficult to find)

PRE-DEPARTURE CHECKLIST

The following list consists of suggestions for you to consider as you prepare to live outside the United States for two years. Not all items will be relevant to everyone, and the list does not include everything you should make arrangements for.

Family
- Notify family that they can call the Peace Corps' Counseling and Outreach Unit at any time if there is a critical illness or death of a family member (24-hour telephone number: 1-855-855-1961, then press 2; or directly at 202-692-1470).

- Give the Peace Corps On the Home Front handbook to family and friends.

Passport/Travel
- Forward to the Peace Corps travel office all paperwork for the Peace Corps passport and visas.

- Verify that your luggage meets the size and weight limits for international travel.

- Obtain a personal passport if you plan to travel after your service ends. (Your Peace Corps passport will expire three months after you finish your service, so if you plan to travel longer, you will need a regular passport.)

Medical/Health
- Complete any needed dental and medical work.

- If you wear glasses, bring two pairs.

- Arrange to bring a three-month supply of all medications (including birth control pills) you are currently taking.

Insurance
- Make arrangements to maintain life insurance coverage.

- Arrange to maintain supplemental health coverage while you are away. (Even though the Peace Corps is responsible for your health care during Peace Corps service overseas, it is advisable for people who have pre-existing conditions to arrange for the continuation of their supplemental health coverage. If there is a lapse in coverage, it is often difficult and expensive to be reinstated.)

- Arrange to continue Medicare coverage if applicable.

Personal Papers
- Bring a copy of your certificate of marriage or divorce.

Voting
- Register to vote in the state of your home of record. (Many state universities consider voting and payment of state taxes as evidence of residence in that state.)

- Obtain a voter registration card and take it with you overseas.

- Arrange to have an absentee ballot forwarded to you overseas.

Personal Effects
- Purchase personal property insurance to extend from the time you leave your home for service overseas until the time you complete your service and return to the United States.

Financial Management
- Keep a bank account in your name in the U.S.

- Obtain student loan deferment forms from the lender or loan service.

- Execute a Power of Attorney for the management of your property and business.

- Arrange for deductions from your readjustment allowance to pay alimony, child support, and other debts through the Office of Volunteer Financial Operations at 855.855.1961, extension 1770.

- Place all important papers—mortgages, deeds, stocks, and bonds—in a safe deposit box or with an attorney or other caretaker.

CONTACTING PEACE CORPS HEADQUARTERS

This list of numbers will help connect you with the appropriate office at Peace Corps headquarters to answer various questions. You can use the toll-free number and extension or dial directly using the local numbers provided. Be sure to leave the toll-free number and extensions with your family so they can contact you in the event of an emergency.

Peace Corps Headquarters Toll-free Number: 855.855.1961, Press 1 or the Ext. # (see below)

Peace Corps' Mailing Address: Peace Corps Headquarters
    11   11 20th Street, NW
    Washin   gton, DC 20526

For Questions About:	Staff:	Toll-Free Ext:	Direct/Local Number:
Responding to an Invitation:	Office of Placement	x1840	202.692.1840
Country Information:	Angela Glenn 202.692.2316 Desk Officer / Botswana and Zambia botswana@peacecorps.gov		
Plane Tickets, Passports, Visas, or other travel matters: CW	T SATO Travel	x1170	202.692.1170
Legal Clearance:	Office of Placement	x1840	202.692.1840
Medical Clearance and Forms Processing (includes dental): Screening	Nurse	x1500	202.692.1500
Medical Reimbursements (handled by a subcontractor):			800.818.8772
Loan Deferments, Taxes, Financial Operations:		x1770	202.692.1770
Readjustment Allowance Withdrawals, Power of Attorney, Staging (Pre-Departure Orientation), and Reporting Instructions: Office	of Staging	x1865	202.692.1865

Note: You will receive comprehensive information (hotel and flight arrangements) three to five weeks prior to departure. This information is not available sooner.

Family Emergencies (to get information to a Volunteer overseas) *24 hours:* Counseling	&	x1470	202.692.1470
Outreach	Unit		

www.ingramcontent.com/pod-product-compliance
Lightning Source LLC
Chambersburg PA
CBHW081803280526
45789CB00008B/2978